I0752580

"To my little brother Sang, who always stands by me, with kindness at his very heart." X B

"To Methuly and Meili, my little bundles of joy and love." Hiruni

Illustrations by Hiruni Kariyawasam

HB : 978-3-912587-09-8
PB : 978-3-912587-00-5

Different Kind Of Bear

Written by Xuan Blooming
Illustrated by Hiruni Kariyawasam

The sky changed colour. All Momo saw was smoke. Orange light danced in the bamboo trees taking Momo's home away.

"We need to go now, Momo.
Before the fire takes our house too."
Mummy waited in the little boat.
Daddy gave Momo a gentle push.
Hop!
And Momo's family left
forever.

They sailed to a new land far, far away.

Momo held Mummy's paw a little tighter.
"They look very different..."
Daddy smiled. "I'm sure they are kind — "

"Let's see
if we can find
a new place
to live."

Some of the brown bears smiled and waved.

Others just **stared.**

"They look very different..."

Momo's eyes were wide with wonder at all the **marvellous** sights and sounds.

"Hello, little fish."

"Momo really loves this place,"
Daddy said to Mummy.

Momo couldn't stop giggling
as he explored the beautiful meadow.

"I think we should stay here
and make a new **home**,"
Mummy said softly.

So they began a new life
in this peaceful spot
near Brown Bear Town.

Momo's house was finally ready.

"Can we invite **everyone** to come and see our new home?"

"That's a **wonderful** idea!"

When the brown bears visited, some smiled at the pretty lanterns but others laughed at them.

The young brown bears did not talk to Momo. No one asked him to play.

On Momo's first day of school, he was **excited!**
But also a little scared. “Do you think they'll like me?”
“Of course Momo Muffin, because you are a kind boy.”

Daddy walked Momo to school.
He gave Momo a big hug and whispered,
"It will be okay, little one. Be **brave.**"

Momo took a deep **breath** and walked through the school gate carrying Daddy's words like a **secret** in his heart.

Momo held his hands
in front of his chest.
He looked so different to
everyone else.
His tummy felt **tight**...

Momo walked into the classroom.
The other kids were busy laughing and whispering.
Momo clutched his backpack a little tighter,
but Mrs Brown Bear's smile made it easier.

DING-A-LING-A-LING!

On the playground bench,
Momo opened his lunchbox.
Dumplings!
His favourite.

Dip, dip... eat, eat...
Dip, dip... eat, eat...
He enjoyed every bite.

Maybe this day wasn't so bad after all.

A group of classmates stopped by Momo's bench.

"What's that?"

"Is it a cotton ball?"

They had never seen **dumplings** before.

"Momo's eating cotton balls!"

They all laughed.

Momo looked down at his lunchbox, holding it close.

"I wish
my fur was like
everyone else's."

"You are special just as you are, son.
What makes you **extra** special is your **kind** heart."

"Daddy,
can being kind change the way
people see us?"
"Yes, Momo Muffin!
Being kind is the most important
thing in life!"
Suddenly,
they heard voices crying for help.

"Help! Help! Bees!"

"Arrrgh!"

"Owww!"

"Someone, help! Please!"

Momo had an idea!
He grabbed a stick.

"Bees don't like **smoke!**"

Daddy helped him to
light the stick.

Momo froze...

He shut his eyes tight.

For a moment
all he saw was smoke and
orange light dancing
in the bamboo trees.

But the brown bears
needed him now...

"This way!"
Momo shouted.
"Follow me!"

He ran ahead
and the brown bears
ran after him.

Splash!

The bees slid away.

"Are you all okay?"

"Yes!"

"Thank you, Momo."

It felt so good to **be kind!**

"Are you turning into a tree?" Momo asked.
"Shhh... Don't blow my cover," Daddy whispered.
First, Momo burst into fits of giggles, then they all laughed together.

"Let's welcome the new family to our town!"
Bear Town

"We were so busy noticing how different they looked we did not see how **kind** they are."

Everyone helped Momo's family feel at home in their new town.

"Can you teach me how to make dumplings please?"

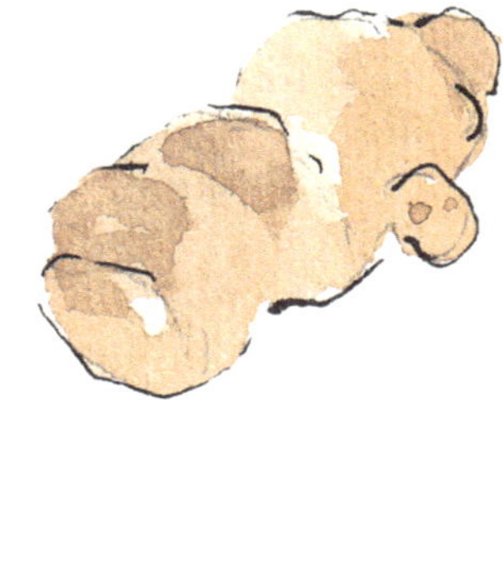

Momo's Mummy's Dumpling Recipe

1. Make the Dough

- In a big bowl, mix 2 cups of plain flour with a pinch of salt.
- Slowly add ¾ cup of warm water, a little at a time, and stir.
- Keep mixing until the dough comes together and feels soft.
- Knead the dough with your hands for about 5 minutes.
- Cover it with a clean cloth and let it rest for 15 minutes.

2. Make the Filling

In a bowl, mix ground pork or ground chicken with:

- A handful of finely chopped Chinese cabbage.
- 1 teaspoon sesame oil.
- 1 teaspoon soy sauce (optional).
- A small bit of grated ginger.
- A pinch of salt and black pepper.
- Stir everything together until well mixed.

3. Wrap the Dumplings

- Roll the dough into a log shape and cut it into small pieces.
- Flatten each piece into a small circle (you can use your hands or a rolling pin).
- Place a spoonful of filling in the middle.
- Fold the dough over the filling and pinch the edges to seal it tight.

(Tip: Press the edges like little waves or folds to make them pretty!).

4. Cook the Dumplings

- Bring a big pot of water to a boil.
- Gently drop the dumplings in, one at a time.
- Stir gently so they don't stick.
- When the dumplings float to the top, cook for another 1—2 minutes.
- Use a spoon to take them out carefully.
- Let them cool a little, they're hot inside!

5. Make a Dipping Sauce (Optional)

Mix together:

- Soy sauce.
- A few drops of vinegar (apple or rice vinegar).
- A slice of fresh ginger.
- A little sesame oil.

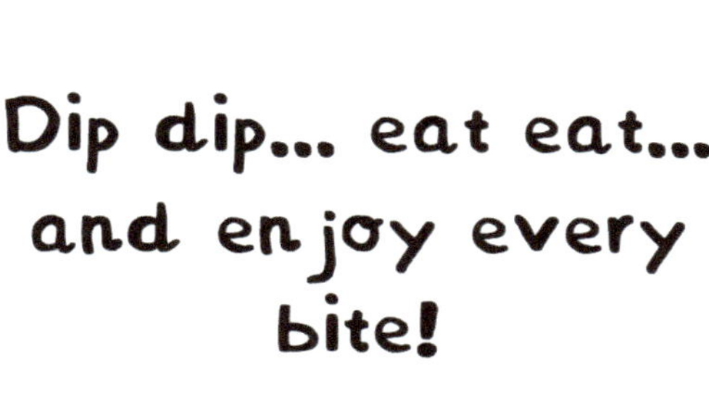

www.ingramcontent.com/pod-product-compliance
Lightning Source LLC
LaVergne TN
LVHW070201110826
845147LV00002B/469
9783912587005